ESSENTIAL **DK** MANAGERS

MANAGING
YOUR CAREER

REBECCA TEE

W9-BHJ-949

LONDON, NEW YORK, MUNICH,
MELBOURNE, AND DELHI

Senior Editor Jacky Jackson
Senior Art Editor Sarah Cowley
US Editors Margaret Parrish, Gary Werner
DTP Designer Rajen Shah
Production Controller Michelle Thomas

Managing Editor Adèle Hayward
Managing Art Editor Marianne Markham
Category Publisher Stephanie Jackson

Produced for Dorling Kindersley by

COOLING BROWN
9–11 High Street, Hampton
Middlesex TW12 2SA

Creative Director Arthur Brown
Senior Editor Amanda Lebentz
Designer Caroline Marklew
Editor Lorraine Turner

First American Edition, 2002

02 03 04 05 10 9 8 7 6 5 4 3 2 1

Published in the United States by
DK Publishing, Inc.
375 Hudson St.
New York, New York 10016

Library of Congress Cataloging-in-Publication Data
Tee, Rebecca.
   Managing your career / Rebecca Tee
   p.cm.-- (Essential managers)
Includes index.
ISBN 0-7894-8951-1 (alk. paper)
   1. Career development. I. Title. II. Series.

HD5381 .T2378 2002
650.14--dc21   2002022961

Reproduced by Colourscan, Singapore
Printed and bound in Hong Kong by Wing King Tong

See our complete product line at

www.dk.com

CONTENTS

INTRODUCTION

The ability to maintain a dynamic career path and develop a portfolio of skills and achievements is a must for managers. Managing Your Career shows you how to build on past experience and maximize opportunities to achieve success and fulfillment in your working life. From reviewing your current situation to exploring career options, monitoring development, and handling crises and change, all the key aspects of effective career planning are covered. With 101 practical tips scattered throughout, and self-assessment exercises that enable you to evaluate how well you have managed your career to date, this is an invaluable pocket reference for every ambitious manager.

MAPPING THE FUTURE

Effective planning is at the heart of career success. Assess your position now, decide where you want to be, and then use your experience to help you map the best route for the future.

WHY MANAGE YOUR CAREER?

Success and happiness at work are rarely achieved by chance. Recognize that by taking a proactive approach to managing your career, you are more likely to realize your ambitions, do justice to your skills, and stay gainfully employed.

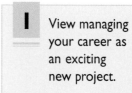

1 View managing your career as an exciting new project.

2 Give planning your career the time and effort it deserves.

MAKING WISE CHOICES

To make the most of all the career choices that face you during your working life, be clear about your goals, alert to opportunities, and quick to make key decisions when necessary. Effective planning will help you be prepared and focused, so that when you need to, you can make the right choices. Nobody wants to look back on their career at retirement and wish they had taken a different path or done things another way.

- A career can be likened to a journey: if that journey is to be a purposeful expedition rather than an aimless one, it will need to be managed well.
- The degree of satisfaction you gain from your work is under your own control.

3 Concentrate on career opportunities.

GAINING A SENSE OF PURPOSE

The most successful career paths have good planning, a sense of direction, and clear milestones along the way. A career path needs to be flexible but it should always be structured. If you have a "map" of your intended route, you can make sure that all the activities in your working life help further your aims and give you a sense of purpose. Managing your career does not mean closing your mind to luck and chance, but involves talking and thinking about your career in a methodical way. This will help you gain further insights and recognize any opportunities as they arise, so that you can make the most of them.

MAKING THE MOST OF YOUR EXPERIENCE

It is rare to know from your first experience of work where you want to go next in your career. Often people find out what suits them over time, learning from their reactions to different positions, environments, roles, and responsibilities. Actively managing your career will help you use all your experience effectively, so that you avoid repeating less successful events and maximize your satisfaction with your working life. You will be better equipped to foresee situations, make sensible, realistic plans, and act upon them. As a result, you will have more confidence and be clearer about your personal priorities.

4 Be prepared to look back as well as ahead.

Team member reaches milestone in career plan

Manager congratulates team member on promotion

FULFILLING YOUR POTENTIAL ▶

Taking control of your career encourages you to make the most of your capabilities so that you feel challenged and stimulated at work. Achieving career goals also brings a great sense of satisfaction.

UNDERSTANDING CAREER MANAGEMENT

Managing your career is not an option but a necessity in order to halt or prevent career drift. Be proactive in developing your career plan so that you do not miss out on the rewards that more focus, drive, and direction can bring.

5 Note that career management gives you added focus in other areas of life.

QUESTIONS TO ASK YOURSELF

Q What does managing my career mean to me?

Q What is the appeal of looking deeper into this subject?

Q How have I managed my career so far?

Q Which aspects of my career do I think need attention?

Q How would I describe my career outlook?

6 Keep your longer-term career goals private.

CLARIFYING YOUR JOURNEY

Just as you would not set off on a journey without a destination and a general route in mind, so you need to plan in a similar way to make a success of your career. By being clear about how to achieve your goals, you will maximize your chances of success. If you are at all career-minded, then you may already be managing your career to some extent. However, there is always scope to raise your career consciousness through analysis and deliberation.

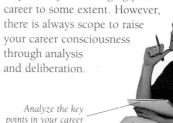

Analyze the key points in your career so far to clarify the way forward

INVESTING IN YOURSELF ▶
The concept of career management may sound daunting, especially if you feel your life is already too busy. But taking time to consider your career in detail is a valuable investment that will enable you to enrich your working life.

WORKING TO A PLAN

Some people have an early career idea that sustains them for years and they dedicate time and effort to pursuing this single goal. What they gain in determination, however, they risk losing in not being adaptable and open to the unexpected. Other people are vague about what they want to achieve and are content to see what turns up in the way of career opportunities. These people benefit from being flexible over their career options but may not progress very fast. The best approach is to work to a structured plan to give you a sense of direction and prevent career drift, but at the same time staying flexible to help you adjust to changes along the way.

7 Aim to be active in the management of your career.

POINTS TO REMEMBER

● The results you achieve depend on the choices and decisions that you make.

● You are responsible for the choices that you make, and you can take control of your work and life balance.

8 Always look ahead, even when you are happy at work and planning seems unnecessary.

▼ BEING AN EFFECTIVE CAREER MANAGER

A career manager has a proactive approach to life, taking the initiative and making things happen. A career drifter has a passive approach, preferring inactivity and taking the easiest option.

CAREER DRIFTER | CAREER MANAGER

Feels out of control

Is unsure of next move

Expects things to "just happen"

Is unclear about the future; feels time is slipping by

Is clear about personal priorities

Has sense of direction

Can see the way forward

Makes the most of experiences

INCREASING YOUR CONTROL

Managing your career does not mean that it will become totally predictable, because there will always be certain factors beyond your control. Relocation of company premises, changes in personnel, fluctuating commercial fortunes, or management restructuring are examples of decisions over which you may not have any influence because they arise from the external environment. There will also be times, such as in unexpected or difficult situations, when you cannot predict or control your own reactions. However, having mapped out your future, you will be able to focus on your longer-term goals during these challenging periods, which can help you stay objective and increase your control.

9 Remember that it is never too early or too late to start managing your career.

WHAT IS A CAREER?

A career is much more than just full-time employment. The following activities should all be considered an important part of your career:

- Permanent or temporary contracts (however short)
- Freelance, consultancy, or self-employment
- Post-retirement activities
- Formal education and training;
- Informal studies or self-taught material
- Development activities (work-based or private learning)
- Voluntary work or any charitable activity
- Political or public representation or involvement
- Hobbies or interests

MAKING CHOICES ▶ IN LATER LIFE

Although George had reached retirement age, he was still able to benefit from managing his career. His years of experience doing voluntary work stood him in good stead when he decided to actively pursue a new position. The church committee was happy to employ George as church sexton, and he continued to enjoy his working life and develop new skills in this role.

CASE STUDY

George had been developing his voluntary activities in his local church over many years. As he approached retirement from his full-time paid employment in a bank, he realized that he was not ready to stop working completely. Approaching the church council, he asked about the possibility of part-time work there. As a result, when he retired from working at the bank at the age of 65, he began a new career as church sexton, caring for the church premises and organizing local activities. Although the salary was much lower than before, he gained great satisfaction from this new career development, which sustained him over the next decade. In addition, he felt that he was making a valuable contribution to the community while still enjoying working, albeit for fewer hours and at a reduced level of energy.

KEEPING UP TO DATE

Changes in the work environment can creep up on you when you are busy living your life. Just think of the developments there have been in communications technology over the last 30 years as a vivid example of the pace of recent inventions. Career management involves paying attention to your own development so that you are continually learning and adding to your experience. By doing this you avoid the risk of being outrun by people whose skills are more recent and up to date.

10 Use every opportunity to learn and develop your skills.

DEFINING KEY ASPECTS OF CAREER MANAGEMENT

KEY AREAS	FACTORS TO CONSIDER
SELF-ANALYSIS Learning about yourself by evaluating your past experience.	● An honest appraisal of your career will help you draw useful conclusions about your strengths and weaknesses. ● Analysis will help you decide where you will "fit" best.
MARKET ASSESSMENT Understanding what is on offer in the employment market.	● A thorough research of the job market is a means of discovering relevant opportunities in your field. ● Consider your own contribution to the world of work.
TARGET-SETTING Establishing what you want to achieve and when.	● Setting targets will give you more focus. ● Once you have set targets, you can plan the steps needed to achieve them so that you progress smoothly.
CHANGE MANAGEMENT Tackling employment difficulties when they arise.	● Handling change effectively involves being adaptable but prepared to alter career direction if necessary. ● Involve other people if change is major.
MONITORING Keeping a check on progress toward career goals.	● Holding regular reviewing and planning sessions will ensure that you stay on track. ● Monitor new developments that may affect your career.

ASSESSING YOUR CURRENT SITUATION

We are all at different stages in our lives and you may want to take stock of your present situation because you feel you need to make a change. Check and analyze your progress to see exactly where you are now and what may lay ahead.

11 Know yourself – this is the key to managing your career successfully.

12 Ensure that you understand all the different aspects of your career.

STOPPING TO THINK ▼
Feeling bored or underemployed is a sign that you need to stop, take stock of your current position, and identify how to put underutilized skills to better use.

CHECKING YOUR PROGRESS

Everyone can benefit from checking their career progress. If you are dissatisfied, it makes sense to stop and ask yourself why. Even if everything is going well, it is still a good idea to check that your career path is proceeding properly and that you are doing enough to maintain this progress. By taking stock of your current position, you can identify what to do next. Look at where you have resources to use and where there are gaps to be filled, perhaps by training, mentoring, or a change of career. Is there any aspect of your current position that you would like to change? For example, you may feel that you deserve more financial reward for your effort, a promotion, or a new challenge.

13 Use dissatisfaction to prompt you to plan your career more actively.

ANALYZING YOUR PROGRESS

How did you get to this point in your career? To find out, consider your career in three ways. First, pay more attention to events and changes that have occurred. Second, study closely the experiences you have gone through, so that you can analyze the causes and effects of your own behavior and that of others. Third, evaluate the consequences of particular types of behavior and decisions that you have made. These three tools – attention, analysis, and evaluation – can provide the information you need.

Manager creates new file to log career events

▲ EVALUATING CAREER MOVES

Get into the habit of logging events and career changes as soon as possible. Make a start by analyzing what has happened so far, using your résumé to prompt your memory.

CONSIDERING YOUR CAREER

Log each change or event as it happens

⬇

Analyze how the event has taken place

⬇

Think how present behavior could influence the future

⬇

Use the analysis to direct your future endeavors

14 Analyze the past to help you illuminate the future.

TOP 10 REASONS FOR CAREER REPOSITIONING

Here are some factors that have motivated others to start managing their career. Do any of them relate to you at the moment?

● Facing a crisis
● Reaching a career crossroads
● Having to make a crucial decision
● Recovering from a difficult period
● Needing longer-term changes
● Wanting to improve future prospects
● Looking to match the success of others
● Ending a period of drifting
● Feeling confused and unclear
● Wanting to take more control over all areas of life

GETTING STARTED

Sometimes the most daunting part of a project is simply getting started. Learn to see career management as enjoyable and instructive in its own right, then you will be able to learn from the process as well as focus more sharply on your future.

15 Take charge of your career to make it more satisfying.

QUESTIONS TO ASK YOURSELF

Q In which direction would I like to be heading?

Q Do I have an ideal career destination in mind?

Q How will I make time to manage my career on a regular basis?

Q What resources do I need to help me?

Q What preparations should I be making at this stage?

MAKING A COMMITMENT

As with any project, to succeed you need to commit yourself fully to the idea of what you are doing and acknowledge in advance the changes that may have to be made. It will involve looking at all areas of your life and could have an impact on your private life and implications for your family. Are you prepared to be honest with yourself, to be open to all possibilities, and to be really thorough in your analysis? Making the time, generating the energy, and finding the focus to concentrate on your career may be stretching.

There may also be risks involved, but there will be rewards for those who have an open mind and a willingness to explore their career possibilities. You will soon have another management skill in your portfolio: that of career management.

Clip out any career articles that interest you

◀ **CREATING A CAREER FILE**
Make up a file of your career thoughts and ideas. Collect job advertisements and course information that interest you. Even if these items are not relevant right away, they may be useful later. You are gathering raw material to help you in the planning process ahead. This file may also provide useful data for future job applications.

16 Invest more time in your career in order to achieve greater rewards.

POINTS TO REMEMBER

- You should always be truthful with yourself and about yourself.
- Changing your approach could change the direction that your career takes.
- It may be necessary to change your appearance or your behavior to pursue a career.

CHOOSING YOUR TOOLS

To complete any job effectively, you need the appropriate tools that reflect your own style and personality. Some people prefer to work alone, perhaps using a computer or a book. Some prefer to use a professional adviser, or a close friend, colleague, or peer group. Sometimes a mixture of these will be appropriate. Use whichever tools you feel most comfortable with, provided they help you progress with your analysis and evaluation.

17 Realize that deciding to explore your career requires effort and application.

USING A SPIDER DIAGRAM

A spider diagram is a useful device for making notes about your career. It is a pictorial method that can help you release your creative thinking, make connections between subjects, and see patterns in your thoughts and behavior that may otherwise remain hidden. A diagram is also more memorable than a list.

◀ **CREATING A DIAGRAM**
Start by writing down a topic in the center of the page. Then note your ideas in branch form radiating out from the center. Work clockwise and keep to a few words for each point.

SETTING GOALS AND TARGETS

Thinking about goals involves envisioning where you want to get to and how you intend to get there. An essential first step is to focus on your ultimate aims. Then set key career markers on the way that you can view as your targets.

18 Keep your options open – it is rare to find one perfect career solution.

DEFINING YOUR GOALS

It may feel difficult to be clear about your ultimate career goals at first. However, you do not need to be too definite about them at this stage. Write down the first three things that occur to you as worth aiming for. Be ambitious for yourself, particularly if you are only just starting out in your career. If you are trying to establish new goals as a result of being laid off or an abrupt change in circumstances, you may initially feel uncertain or unconfident about the future. In these situations it is still important to be determined and to avoid allowing a difficult experience to hold you back.

Tells friend that she wants to be her own boss

CLARIFYING ▶ YOUR GOALS

Discuss your goals with a partner or colleague to help you make them as specific as possible. This will make it easier to work toward them. Seek to turn vague goals such as "I want more responsibility", into concrete ones such as "I want to become head of my department".

CONSIDERING BOUNDARIES

Think through the goals you have written down. Ruling out the impractical will save you time and remove distractions. Is changing location out of the question? Will you need to study? If you need to keep earning money while you study, figure out how much you need to live on compared to your present income. This will clarify how flexible you can afford to be. Perhaps distance learning will enable you to continue earning while you learn? Do you have, or plan to have, a family, and does that need to be incorporated into your career management plans?

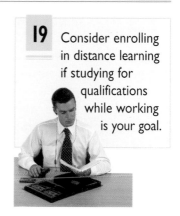

19 Consider enrolling in distance learning if studying for qualifications while working is your goal.

QUESTIONS TO ASK YOURSELF

Q Do I have at least three targets to help me reach each of my goals?

Q Are my targets both ambitious enough and achievable?

Q Have I made a serious undertaking with myself to pursue these goals?

Responds by asking what exactly she wants to do

SETTING TARGETS

Now you have identified some goals, break them down into smaller steps. In this way you will be able to move forward. Suppose you had written down "become a leader in my field." That is unlikely to happen overnight – it will need planning and effort if it is to come true – and several things will need to occur for this career goal to be achieved. You may need to study to a higher level and establish a reputation in clinical work or on the conference circuit. You may need to publish details of your work in academic or professional journals, and you will need to have some original work under your belt. This goal, therefore, has four distinct targets to use as milestones in your career: study, establish a reputation, get published, and produce original work. As you reach each target you will know that you are nearer your goal.

20 Make sure you choose the way of working that feels most comfortable to you.

IDENTIFYING YOUR ASSETS

Assets in career terms include your personality strengths and work achievements. Identify your assets and the skills and knowledge you have accumulated in order to provide a sturdy foundation on which to build your future plans.

21 Ask friends and colleagues for their perceptions of your character.

22 Try to evaluate how others see you to understand your own assets.

DESCRIBING YOUR PERSONAL STYLE

You need to understand the type of person you are to envision where you would best fit into the working world. Think how your friends and colleagues would describe you at your best, and then make a list of your assets. Remember to include any positive feedback you have received during performance reviews and in references and any compliments paid to you by colleagues.

LISTING YOUR ASSETS

Use the following list of assets to help prompt you when creating your own list of attributes that describe your character. Do not worry about ordering or qualifying what you write.

- Able to work alone
- Accurate
- Adaptable
- Alert
- Approachable
- Articulate
- Assertive
- Calm
- Capable
- Cautious
- Collaborator
- Committed
- Competent
- Confident
- Cooperative
- Creative
- Decisive
- Dedicated
- Determined
- Dynamic
- Enthusiastic
- Flexible
- Friendly
- Good at deadlines
- Good manager
- Hardworking
- Humorous
- Innovative
- Lively
- Loyal
- Methodical
- Motivator
- Optimistic
- Organized
- Patient
- Perceptive
- Polite
- Proactive
- Punctual
- Quick to learn
- Reliable
- Responsible
- Self-motivated
- Sensible
- Sensitive
- Serious-minded
- Shows flair
- Steadfast
- Strong
- Tactful
- Thorough
- Versatile

23 Retrace your steps as a useful exercise in learning.

24 View your portfolio as all the elements of your career so far.

ANALYZING YOUR DESCRIPTION

Review your list of assets. Do they all describe similar strengths or do they show a very varied character? Does the list make you think of any particular work environment that would be suitable (or unsuitable) for this kind of person? Are you happy with the picture presented by this list? Do you wish you could add different words? Are there actions you could take to help you expand the list? For example, if you want to be able to add the word "assertive," could you gain more assertiveness through training? Keep a record of the list and your thoughts about it for future reflection.

COMPILING YOUR PORTFOLIO

Your portfolio should include all your skills, knowledge, and achievements gained from all your employment endeavors so far. It is important to remember all that you have achieved so that you can build up an accurate chronology of your work history for your portfolio.

List the positions you have held, the places in which you have been based, and the skills you have learned. Try to fill in any gaps or sketchy details, such as missing months. Ascertaining exactly where an assignment took place, for example, may help you remember how you felt about being there

▼ RECORDING YOUR EXPERIENCES
In a notebook, using perhaps a page for each year, enter all the different activities on which you have spent time, the skills and knowledge you have gained, and where you have been based.

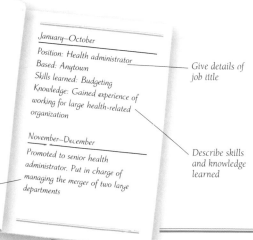

January–October
Position: Health administrator
Based: Anytown
Skills learned: Budgeting
Knowledge: Gained experience of working for large health-related organization

— *Give details of job title*

November–December
Promoted to senior health administrator. Put in charge of managing the merger of two large departments

— *Describe skills and knowledge learned*

Record any achievements

EVALUATING YOUR PORTFOLIO

Exploring the choices and changes you have made in the past can highlight trends and connections that have affected you. Use this new insight to see the most effective way forward, minimize negative patterns, and maximize useful connections.

25 Try to identify any recurring themes or unexpected links.

26 Read old diaries to find out how you felt during different work phases.

LOOKING BACK

Now that you have all the information about your employment history in your portfolio, analyze how you felt about each stage. This will enable you to be clear about which elements you want to maximize and which to minimize. Constructing a timeline of your level of satisfaction at each point can help you locate patterns and themes in what you have done in the past – some may have been beneficial to your career, while others may have held you back. Plot the patterns on a graph to show the ups and downs of each stage. Accuracy is not as important as the relative high and low points. Think around the job to include the peer group, managers, and the team with which you worked most closely.

◀ **PLOTTING A TIMELINE**
Create a timeline to represent your career path. Can you see any patterns emerging about where and when you were most and least satisfied? What was happening in your life then? Analyze and learn from the material that emerges.

Temporary contract | *Training course* | *Laid off* | *New job*

High

Career Satisfaction

Low

0   1   2   3   4   5
Time (Years)

Motherhood career break | *Continuing education*

USING PHOTOGRAPHS AS PROMPTS

Photographs can be a helpful indication of your state of mind at different times. Sometimes the camera captures expressions that we are not aware of. Collect old shots of you at different stages in your career. How do you look in each – on top of things, full of pride, and with a sense of worth? Perhaps there are periods when you seem glum or depressed, where you are not taking as much care of yourself as you should? Ask friends and family if they remember you during these different phases to see if their recollections tally with your own. You could rank the photographs in order of happy appearance and see if this ties in with your memory of the satisfaction you were gaining at work at the time. Work takes up such a major slice of our lives that you will often find this to be the case.

◀ **LOOKING FOR CLUES**
Study old photo albums for insights into how your career has affected your emotional well-being.

LEARNING FROM THE HIGH POINTS

The times in your career when you have felt most successful will be clear indicators of situations that played to your strengths. List the happy times, detailing the position you held, the team in which you operated, the resulting achievements, and the way you felt about each situation. Which strengths were you exhibiting at which time? Assess whether the type of role you played made a difference to the way you performed. Perhaps you were given extra responsibility and lived up to expectations, or perhaps you were working as part of a tightly knit team that brought out the best in you? Or perhaps you enjoyed happy experiences because you were interested in the products or services with which you were involved, or the environment in which you worked.

QUESTIONS TO ASK YOURSELF

Q How do my career peaks and troughs help me plan ahead?

Q Can I identify helpful situations to seek out from now on?

Q Are there scenarios to avoid repeating in the future?

Q Do the answers to the last two questions point to a particular career direction?

27 Try to find reasons for the most successful periods in your career.

UNDERSTANDING THE LOW POINTS

Even in the shortest career you are likely to have spent some time feeling rather uninspired. Examine those periods now to see if they illustrate situations to avoid in the future. Were you working for employers you disliked or within teams that were dysfunctional? What effect did these periods have on you and on your general morale? Perhaps the culture of the sector in which the job was located did not match your values? How did these differences make you feel, and what, if anything, did you do about it?

28 Analyze the low points in your career and the reasons for them.

▼ LEARNING FROM LOW POINTS

In this example, a manager's experience of a festering dispute between two colleagues proves a valuable learning aid. He now encourages his team to discuss their differences and find ways of resolving them.

Team member freely airs his opinion

Manager acts as arbiter

Team member expresses her point of view

◄ GAINING FROM EXPERIENCE

Bill's experience of working for a manufacturing organization was a very positive one. He felt integrated into the company and was determined to learn as much as possible before moving on. Nancy learned that working in isolation was demotivating for her and decided to look for a new job before her morale fell any further.

CASE STUDY

Bill, a sales manager, and Nancy, an office manager, both worked for the same manufacturing organization. Bill enjoyed his job immensely, and ran a close-knit team that strove hard to reach its sales targets. He was eager to build on his success within the organization for a couple of years, after which he planned to realize his ambitions by moving on to gain wider experience of sales management in a different working environment.

Nancy was miserable in her role as office manager. She felt stultified by the lack of interest shown in her work by her boss and often felt remote from the organization because it was difficult to see how her team contributed to the end product. There were no challenging sales targets to reach and no contact with the organization's customers. She could feel her morale falling and her confidence slowly ebbing away and knew that she must move to a new job soon.

RECOGNIZING PATTERNS

When situations crop up again and again, even if not in exactly the same form, we can learn from them. These patterns may help us move forward, or they may block our progress. Can you see any patterns in your past? Have there been several similar incidents or working relationships? Perhaps people consistently relate to you in a certain manner or perhaps you keep finding yourself in similar situations? It may be the first time that you have looked back at your career in this way. Try to think about any aspect of your own behavior that may contribute to the frequency of the pattern occurring.

29 Be productive in your analysis – avoid regretting past behavior.

30 Move on if you cannot change or learn from recurring patterns.

DOS AND DON'TS

✔ Do make sure you reward yourself for your successes.

✔ Do ask your friends, partner, and colleagues for feedback on your work–life balance.

✘ Don't focus on your mistakes and ignore your successes.

✘ Don't underestimate the value of coaching in helping you clarify your objectives.

▼ SUMMARIZING YOUR EVALUATION

Write down what you have learned from your analysis to help increase your understanding. Think about key areas for improvement and then record what action you plan to take and by when, so that you feel you have committed to it in writing.

Joe Smith: ANALYSIS

Mistakes	Running restaurant with my brother – I jumped in too quickly.
Disappointments	Two years of low income and stressful family relationships.
Learning points	However exciting the career prospect, I must thoroughly evaluate every project solely on business grounds before I commit to it.
Areas for development	I need to improve my financial and budgeting analysis and marketing skills so that I am able to assess the business feasibility of projects more confidently.
Action	Look into college courses and aim to start studying part-time by end of year.

Previous difficulties caused by eagerness for new projects

Learned to temper enthusiasm with harder-edged business analysis

EXPLORING THE POSSIBILITIES

Any dreams you have had of your perfect career should not be ignored. If you have imagined career paths that would bring you great satisfaction, consider them now in more detail to check their feasibility. They may be more achievable than you thought.

31 Ask family and friends what kind of job they think would suit you.

32 Take time out to revisit forgotten plans and dream up some solutions.

DARING TO DREAM

Managing your career involves exploring dreams. Do you have a wish to improve your qualifications or an old hankering to follow a career that requires specialized skills? Perhaps you dreamed of being a ballet dancer or a brain surgeon, or following the same career path as a friend? Or you may have a few vague ideas but do not know enough to do anything about them at this stage. Be explicit about each idea and explore what there is to be gained from taking any of them further.

TAKING THE LONG VIEW

Every job has periods of stagnation. Try to avoid thinking that total happiness and continual movement forward should be the norm. If there is still scope for progress later, treading water for a time is fine. For example, you may find that the results for your division are poorer than expected. If you know that a new computer sales system and a thorough retraining package are soon to be introduced, it may be better to wait and see what happens. Think about your career over a period of a year. It takes a good six months in any new position to feel really confident about it.

POINTS TO REMEMBER

- Beware of acting hastily. It is often a good idea to bide your time until a conclusion is clearer.
- Appealing career ideas may hint at undeveloped talents.
- Having decided that a career possibility is not for you, the idea should be discarded so that you are able to move on.
- If there is an activity you love, consider whether there is any way of fitting it into your working life.

PUSHING BACK THE BOUNDARIES

Spending time on the activities you like best can seem like an expensive luxury. However, if there are activities that you have always wanted to spend time on, it is worth considering ways of bringing them into your present working life. Many people have creative abilities that have to take a back seat because of the need to seek gainful employment. To achieve a more satisfying balance in your life, look at how you can devote more time to doing what you enjoy most.

33 Think what you want to see when you look back in 10 years' time.

Studies interior design and works freelance to gain experience

DREAM	OPTIONS	ACTION
To run my own interior design and decorating business	Look at part-time college courses and career prospects after graduation	Enroll in course and help friends with redecorating to test commitment

Employee reads design magazines to help with research

▲ **REALIZING A DREAM**
If you wish to pursue a new career direction, research any training needed to obtain necessary qualifications and look at the prospects. You can then plan your action accordingly.

DOS AND DON'TS

✔ Do think back to your earliest innovative career ideas.

✔ Do reflect on the work of people you know.

✔ Do consider occupations that you have heard of or read about.

✘ Don't be constrained by your past work history.

✘ Don't rule out options that sound unlikely without thinking about whether they could be made to happen.

✘ Don't include anything totally unrealistic.

FORMING CONCLUSIONS

Think about what you want to achieve in the future and create a plan of action to help you plot the way forward. Do you need to find out more about career possibilities? You may need to gather more information. To help you understand your path, be clear and honest about your own motivation. What do you want to achieve in 10 years' time? Money, an expert reputation, increased status, or an improved work-life balance?

ASSESSING YOUR CAREER MANAGEMENT

*E*valuate your current career management by working through this simple questionnaire. Be as honest as you can and answer with the first response that comes into your mind. If your answer is "disagree," mark Option 1; if it is "agree," mark Option 4; and so on. Add your scores together, then refer to the Analysis to see what that score represents.

OPTIONS

1 Disagree

2 Slightly disagree

3 Slightly agree

4 Agree

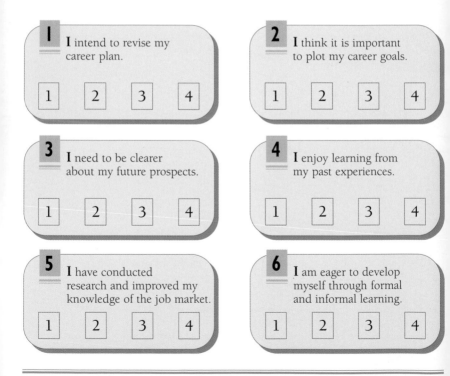

1 I intend to revise my career plan.

| 1 | 2 | 3 | 4 |

2 I think it is important to plot my career goals.

| 1 | 2 | 3 | 4 |

3 I need to be clearer about my future prospects.

| 1 | 2 | 3 | 4 |

4 I enjoy learning from my past experiences.

| 1 | 2 | 3 | 4 |

5 I have conducted research and improved my knowledge of the job market.

| 1 | 2 | 3 | 4 |

6 I am eager to develop myself through formal and informal learning.

| 1 | 2 | 3 | 4 |

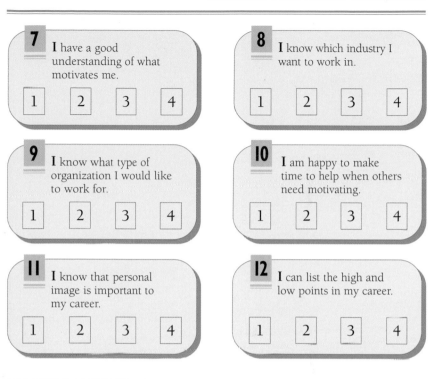

7 I have a good understanding of what motivates me.

1   2   3   4

8 I know which industry I want to work in.

1   2   3   4

9 I know what type of organization I would like to work for.

1   2   3   4

10 I am happy to make time to help when others need motivating.

1   2   3   4

11 I know that personal image is important to my career.

1   2   3   4

12 I can list the high and low points in my career.

1   2   3   4

ANALYSIS

Add up your score and check your career management skills by referring to the evaluation below. Identify your weakest areas and refer to the relevant sections in this book to help you refine your skills.

12–26: You seem halfhearted about your prospects. You may want to come back to this subject later when the benefits of career management are clearer.

27–39: You are learning about career management and can analyze your experience and assess your present position. Think about where you are aiming in order to complete the process.

40–48: You can see how your career will be improved by thorough planning and continual personal development. You will soon be in a position to maximize opportunities that come your way.

EXPLORING CAREER OPTIONS

It is important to be aware of the kind of work that is currently available in the marketplace. Do as much research as possible and use your network of friends and contacts.

RESEARCHING AND NETWORKING

Many jobs are never advertised but are filled through word of mouth. Find out how the companies concerned recruit their staff and how you can access networks that can help you track down, and be considered for, these job opportunities.

34 Be supportive of others – you may need their help later in life.

35 Read reference books or annuals to gain an overview of current key industry players.

ACCESSING INFORMATION

Having accurate information about companies, employment opportunities, and the job market is vital for working out your next career move. Research carefully the companies and markets in which you have an interest. Make your research formal and deliberate, and give yourself plenty of time in which to do it. Use your contacts with family, friends, colleagues, and associates to give you further insight into potential job opportunities.

APPRAISING THE MARKET

Find out as much as you can about the business that interests you. Read newspapers and magazines, tune into television or radio documentaries, surf the internet, or attend industry seminars and exhibitions to keep informed. Stay abreast of current market conditions and future forecasts that might affect job availability. If you are eager to work in the nonprofit sector, for example, you need to be aware that government funding can have a big impact on job vacancies in this area because the level of funding fluctuates with different economic and political priorities.

POINTS TO REMEMBER

● Finding out about an organization's working environment and culture can pay dividends when you apply for a job.

● Reading material published by organizations in which you are interested will help you find out about current priorities, policies, and plans.

● Researching professional or trade association websites and publications can illuminate unfamiliar areas of work.

TALKING TO AGENCIES ▶
Employment agencies have their finger on the pulse of demand and supply. Ask for an interview and check out the state of the market in their skill area.

Specialist describes a thriving market – but only for people with the right skills

36 Access websites of organizations to see how they project themselves.

CHOOSING YOUR APPROACH

Since organizations and sectors tend to recruit staff in different ways, you need to find out how and where they recruit, what they are looking for, and how you can apply for any vacancies. Large corporations, for example, rely mainly on press or website advertisements or recruitment agencies. Smaller firms may be more open to approaches from individuals, particularly if the person seems to meet a current need and can be hired without recruitment costs. Some organizations prefer to fill vacancies on a temporary or contract basis, which allows them more time to recruit permanent staff.

37 Monitor job sites on the internet to find out where the opportunities are.

JUSTIFYING NETWORKING

Networking may sound a cold and callous way of using your friends and colleagues to further your career, but it is actually a sensible extension to your research methods. Friends have probably inquired about your work or asked you to keep your eyes open for future job vacancies at your company in the past. Most of us are only too pleased to help others in this way. Often the information you gain through networking is about more than just a specific vacancy, and this may turn out to have a greater relevance than you think.

38 Think like a careers adviser – ask people about their working lives.

Even friends' networks may prove useful

FRIENDS'
CONTACTS

REMOTE
CONNECTIONS

CONTACTS

ASSOCIATES

FRIENDS

FAMILY

Family and friends are the most immediate sources of networking

▲ LISTING CONTACTS
Begin by listing all the people you know who may have access to information about the kind of career that interests you. Think of all your personal and work contacts – these are your network.

ASSESSING THE JOB MARKET

Use newspapers to help you with your assessment of the job market. Look at the job vacancy advertisements to get an idea of buoyant sectors and information about the standards required for each job. Study the financial and business pages for a more in-depth focus on longer-term employment and performance trends in different sectors. Take time to digest specialized or feature articles that can give a wider picture of the world of work.

◀ READING THE PAPERS
Choose newspapers with the largest number of relevant job vacancies and study them carefully, reading articles that you would usually pass over.

DOS AND DON'TS

✔ Do think about all your contacts, past and present, and be creative about how they could be of assistance.

✔ Do show appropriate gratitude when people try to help you.

✔ Do give people the chance to say "no" should they feel it would be difficult to help you for some reason.

✘ Don't feel embarrassed to approach people on your networking list — think of it as seeking and offering information.

✘ Don't overload the same people all the time — no one likes to feel responsible for another's career progress.

✘ Don't forget to support other people who may need assistance from you.

39 Add names to your network whenever possible.

40 Show an interest in others so that interaction is not all one-way.

41 Use social gatherings to meet new contacts and expand your nework of contacts.

USING YOUR NETWORK

Think about how the people you have identified in your network can help you. Depending on the nature of your association and their current position, you can plan how to enlist their support. Perhaps they worked for a competing organization? If so, they might be able to give you inside information about the fortunes of key players in the sector and current priorities and policies. Perhaps they work for the company you want to move to? Begin by calling and just having a chat. Follow up with an informal lunch to take the discussion further.

◀ **NETWORK LUNCHING**
By networking, Royston succeeded in moving one step ahead of the competition and getting the job of his dreams. He and his ex-colleague had always gotten along, and Royston knew that he would be happy to help him advance his career.

CASE STUDY

Royston wanted to find a job in a national broadcasting organization. He knew that all its vacancies were advertised in the press but he was eager to get any advantage that he could. He discovered that an ex-colleague now worked for the same corporation. They arranged to meet, with Royston buying lunch. For the price of a roast beef sandwich and a soda, Royston gained in three ways. The first was that the contact sent him the internal weekly newsletter that detailed all the upcoming job vacancies seven days before they appeared in the national press. Second, his contact told him all about the work atmosphere and how he had obtained his own job. Third, the contact directed him to an article by a key department head, detailing the kind of employees he was seeking. Royston is now working at his dream job in the corporation.

EXAMINING SCOPE AND OPPORTUNITY

To help you find the right career, you need to look at the scope and focus of different employment opportunities. Consider the sector, size, and structure of different workplaces – these may be deciding factors in your choice of employment.

42 Remember that all career exploration is an evolving process.

43 Think which type of organization you would like to be with in 10 years.

EVALUATING SECTORS ▼
If you envision working in manufacturing, monitor the performance of companies within that sector to help you assess which are likely to offer the most opportunity.

CONSIDERING STRUCTURE

Study an organization's management structure to help you identify new opportunities and avoid jobs with little potential for growth. Most organizations have broadly similar management structures, whatever their size or sector. Senior management has a strategic overview of the essential business, and reporting to them are the departmental or divisional managers who set the day-to-day priorities. Middle managers or supervisors report to these managers and have an overview of the teams carrying out the work.

MONITORING SECTORS

Monitor the fortunes of sectors and the companies within them. Your options will be more limited in a declining sector and vice versa. A real growth area in recent years has been the service sector. Read the metropolitan and business sections of newspapers to assess current economic successes and failures.

CONSIDERING THE SIZE OF AN ORGANIZATION

SIZE	ADVANTAGES	DISADVANTAGES
SMALL	● Freedom to make decisions. ● Involvement in all aspects of work. ● Liaison with external providers and consultants. ● Direct relationship with clients or customers.	● Your actions and decisions are vital, so your responsibility is greater. ● Family atmosphere but family-type pressures, too. ● Limited scope for progressing up the career ladder.
MEDIUM	● Teamwork is important; close relationship with colleagues. ● Opportunities to see and learn from other disciplines and functions. ● Chance to input your ideas. ● Financial stability.	● Too large to star, too small to allow much opportunity. ● People outside the company are unlikely to have heard of it. ● Less secure employment than with a large organization.
LARGE	● Many career routes may be available. ● More chance of organization's investment in your development. ● Higher salary levels and benefits. ● Has currency in wider employment market when you want to move on.	● Organization may be so large that you feel compartmentalized. ● Less chance of any one individual having an effect on the company. ● Can be difficult to gain recognition or a sense of achievement.

CHOOSING PUBLIC OR PRIVATE SECTORS

The old boundaries between public and private sectors are becoming increasingly blurred. Private companies support schools and hospitals; trade unions and businesses work in partnership; government and corporations cooperate on national initiatives, and the nonprofit sector is eager to learn best business practice. Public sector experience is now highly valued by companies that sell goods and services to schools and hospitals. It is important to understand the differences and similarities between the sectors to enable you to talk confidently at job interviews about the environment of your choice.

QUESTIONS TO ASK YOURSELF

Q Can I imagine myself doing something completely different?

Q Do I have a business idea that could work?

Q Do I want to move into a new sector or to a different size of organization?

Q Do I want to move higher up the management ladder?

Q Would I take a pay cut to work in a nonprofit organization where I would be making a contribution to society?

USING THE JOB SEARCH PROCESS

An analysis of the job market should be followed up with more detailed research into individual jobs. Go through the process of applying for vacancies to help you learn much more about the type of role that might best suit you.

44 Rehearse your presentation before you have an interview.

TARGETING YOUR RESEARCH

> **Find vacancies that interest you and request job descriptions**

> **Study the details of each job to assess your suitability for the role**

> **Outline the contribution you could make and plan how to present your case**

> **Compose your job application, making it as impressive as you can**

> **If there is more that you need to know about the job, plan questions to ask**

ANALYZING VACANCIES

Once you have looked at the job opportunities available and assessed the suitability of different business sectors, target individual vacancies in order to find out more. If you find a vacancy that really appeals to you, dissect the advertisement and any information that the employer sends you. Find out as much as possible about the organization and its products or services. List the key points of the role to establish what the employer is looking for. By going through this selection process you will discover whether you are interested in the job, or perhaps even form a very different impression of the vacancy.

DOS AND DON'TS

✔ Do apply for vacancies that stretch you beyond your present level.

✘ Don't build up your hopes too high over any particular job.

✔ Do maintain a positive attitude, concentrating on your strengths.

✘ Don't hold back at an interview if you are enthusiastic.

✔ Do ask for feedback; it can help you learn from a disappointment.

✘ Don't get despondent if and when you experience rejection.

ASSESSING SUITABILITY

Job applications may take time, effort, and a substantial investment of self-confidence, but it is always worth applying for jobs you think would really suit you. Start by matching the detail of the vacancy to yourself. Do you have the relevant experience, attributes, and personality to claim this job for your own? You may decide not to continue with the application once you have considered all the information, or you may be able to improve your suitability by stressing your transferable skills. For example, if you have not managed large teams before you could emphasize your leadership role in complex projects and your varied responsibilities.

45 Show eagerness in an interview, even if you are not yet sure about the job.

Candidate learns that role is far more diverse than she thought

Manager explains what job entails

KEEPING ▶ AN OPEN MIND
Approach every interview seriously, even when you are not sure that you want the job. The selection process may lead you to change your mind.

46 Keep records of all your applications and interviews.

47 Tell a company if you decide not to take the application process further.

FORMING YOUR OPINION

If you are invited to an interview, use this chance to learn more about the job and broaden your research into finding the role that is right for you. Attending the interview will enable you to look at the environment, meet people with whom you will be working, hear more about the job concerned, and seek answers to any outstanding issues. You can then make a final judgment. If you are offered the job and you liked what you saw, you can accept with confidence. If you decide not to go further with the application, view the experience as good practice. If you are not offered the position, use the process to improve future endeavors.

EXPLORING SELF-EMPLOYMENT

More and more people are considering self-employment, especially if they need to fit their work around other areas of their lives, such as family commitments. Look at the key issues of this style of working to see if it has any attractions for you.

48 Use your business networks to lead you to potential new clients.

49 Involve your family in the development of your plans.

50 Limit your initial financial investment and keep money-related paperwork.

GOING IT ALONE

Self-employment offers varied job opportunities. It is particularly appealing to parents because it gives them more flexibility to combine working and bringing up children, although it is not an easy option. Self-employment makes it easier to embark upon a new career and on very different terms from those of the employee. There is also the possibility that you may be able to develop a sideline into your main source of income. Do you have an interest in something that you think could earn you money? Look at the local economy to see which services are in short supply.

FRANCHISING

This is a halfway house between self-employment and working for an employer: a company gives you the right to sell its product or service in return for a regular payment. Examples include makeup sold at home, fast-food restaurants, and coffee shops. You do have to pay money up front to buy into them, and they can be expensive, so make sure the franchising company is reputable. Seek advice from statutory authorities that oversee the issue of franchises, relevant local government departments, and consumer protection agencies before you commit yourself. If possible, talk to other franchise holders before making a decision.

CONSIDERING SELF-EMPLOYMENT

BENEFITS	DISADVANTAGES

BENEFITS

- Able to work at your own pace.
- Can choose not to work or mix work and domestic responsibilities.
- May decide how far to pursue business goals and invest how you want.
- Can set your own rates or fees.
- Able to experiment as you choose.
- Can share resources with others.
- Satisfaction of having control over the product or service.
- Your successes are immediately apparent.
- Work can become more creative and dynamic.

DISADVANTAGES

- Can involve working long hours, difficult to switch off.
- Requires strict self-discipline.
- Feast or famine: it is rare to have a steady stream of income.
- Need to budget carefully and plan the workload.
- Need confidence to sell and justify quality.
- Expected to be working only on each customer's particular job.
- Little financial security (unless purchased).

51 Keep 3 to 6 months' salary saved, just in case.

EXAMINING FEASIBILITY

Ask yourself a series of questions that could form the basis of an eventual business plan. The first considerations are: what would you be selling and do you have any evidence of demand? Successful businesses tend to be demand-led, where they have built up an interest in what they are selling over a period of time. Seek opinions from other people. Ask if they would buy your service or product and how much they would pay. Find out where they usually hear about such products or services. Aim to attract business before spending money on building a business profile, because without sales you will not survive.

Potential small businessman researches local companies

◀ **DOING YOUR RESEARCH**

If you are thinking about self-employment, aim to research the local competition thoroughly. Find out whether your services are likely to be in demand, and what people in the same business are charging.

37

DEVELOPING YOUR CAREER

Career changes happen in stages, but even the most determined job-changer works in a particular role most of the time. Learn how to manage your working life between these changes.

REVIEWING AND PLANNING

Developing your career involves closely monitoring your progress to ensure that future plans are still on track. Hold regular reviewing and planning sessions so that you can assess what you have achieved and what you need to do next.

52 Keep computer files on your career private if writing them at work.

53 Gain other people's perceptions of events at work.

54 Try combining your work reviews with reviews of your life in general.

REVIEWING YOUR WORK

Establish a pattern of regularly reviewing your work in a critical but constructive way. Use this exercise to make plans for the future and learn lessons from the past. It is useful to evaluate your progress after every job change and each work project you have managed or completed. You should be incorporating normal work planning and reviewing as part of your job, but this is adding the personal career element. The results will give you raw material you can use again in future job applications and interviews as well as for your own internal job performance or reviews.

55 Criticize yourself constructively and be generous with self-praise.

Q Can I identify aspects of my work that I would like to experience more frequently?

Q Are there aspects of my work that did not suit me that I could avoid in the future?

Q What made the high or low points of my position significant?

Q Can I improve my present situation by calling on previous experience?

UTILIZING THE PAST

Make the most of your previous experience. Analyze what has happened to you and how you feel about it, and act on it. If possible, talk to other people who were around at the time to get their views on what occurred. You are hired to do a job because you have exhibited some skills in that area in the past. As a result, you may find that you are always given the same kind of work to do, with little possibility of being given something different to try. It is often opportunities outside work that can develop you in new ways and create new talents. Perhaps there are roles in your community, part-time work that could grow into a full-time role, or self-employment opportunities that you could consider? A flexible approach to enhancing the aspects of work that please and excite you can help you maximize your satisfaction with your career.

Manager compiles thoughts on his latest project and what he has learned from it

REVIEWING AND PLANNING EFFECTIVELY

Ask yourself what has happened since your last review

Think how events occurred and how you feel about them

Consider what you would like to happen next

Decide how you will achieve a new goal

▲ RECORDING YOUR CONCLUSIONS
Keep a permanent record of your conclusions either in a specially purchased notebook or wallet file or on a computer. Date and sign your notes to give them a more formal status.

CHOOSING REVIEW DATES

Try to tie in your career reviews with a regular event. Any of the following times may be suitable for you:

- On the first or last day of each month
- As the financial year begins or ends
- At the start or end of each calendar year
- On your birthday
- After some internal changes at work
- After some personal changes

- On the anniversary of starting your present job
- When you are starting a new position or leaving one
- When you are about to start or have just completed a project

---

56 Include new and challenging targets in each career plan.

WRITING YOUR CAREER PLAN

It is best to create a plan that includes both one-year and five-year targets. Write down how you see the future developing. Include some ambitious goals to keep you reaching as far as you can, and nonwork issues too if you want your career plan to cover all your activities. Include something creative or unusual to expand your horizons and keep you trying out new subjects or skill areas. Schedule in some learning too, whether it is a formal course or a less structured program.

MAKING A CAREER PLAN ▼

Here are some of the topics that your plan should cover. Add more according to your own circumstances: a varied plan makes for a varied career.

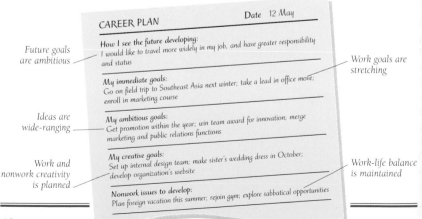

Future goals are ambitious

Ideas are wide-ranging

Work and nonwork creativity is planned

Work goals are stretching

Work-life balance is maintained

CAREER PLAN   Date 12 May

How I see the future developing:
I would like to travel more widely in my job, and have greater responsibility and status

My immediate goals:
Go on field trip to Southeast Asia next winter; take a lead in office move; enroll in marketing course

My ambitious goals:
Get promotion within the year; win team award for innovation; merge marketing and public relations functions

My creative goals:
Set up internal design team; make sister's wedding dress in October; develop organization's website

Nonwork issues to develop:
Plan foreign vacation this summer; rejoin gym; explore sabbatical opportunities

CASE STUDY

Margaret was happy enough in her job as an editor but felt lonely. When she looked back at her previous work history she found that the times when she had felt most fulfilled were when she was working as part of a team at the center of operations. She was unwilling to jeopardize her present position, so she decided instead to look for ways of building the element of teamwork into her future that she felt she was missing. She found her ideal team role outside work through her interest in a campaigning organization. She asked if she could help as a trustee on the organization's management board and was accepted right away. In her new role, she enjoys working on strategic issues and policy, while others direct the organization. She still uses her professional skills to the full in her day job and feels far more fulfilled overall.

USING YOUR CAREER PLAN

Make sure that you check your career plan regularly to see what you have achieved. Check off the targets that you have reached, noting any future work that may need to be done. For example, a work project may need monitoring in the future. Update entries that need further work with altered timescales and revised targets. What has been delaying you on these points? Finally, revisit those items where no action took place. Analyze carefully what went wrong. Perhaps you need to reframe an unrealistic goal, or perhaps you simply ran out of time? Plan how to avoid this during the next period. If the goal is still important to you, include it for another year. Otherwise, delete it and rearrange other aspects of the plan to compensate. Keep old plans to give you a sense of perspective. You will find these records of your past career management very useful when you are completing application forms in the future.

POINTS TO REMEMBER

- All the possibilities should be outlined in order to assess what is feasible.

- Hurdles that could prevent you from achieving your goals need to be identified so that you can plan how to overcome them.

57 Realize that work alone will not fulfill all your needs.

58 Talk through your career plan with family or friends.

BENEFITING FROM PERFORMANCE REVIEWS

Regular performance reviews are essential if you want to keep on top of your career. If reviews are conducted by your employer, learn from them and identify further opportunities to develop. Alternatively, plan to evaluate yourself.

59 Consider how you see your future developing with your employer.

UNDERSTANDING REVIEWS

The best companies will have systems in place to help staff think about their work in terms of how they fit into the organization. A time will be booked with your manager to discuss your work since the last review and to set targets and development activities for the period ahead. Not every organization is so well run, but if you are lucky enough to be offered such an opportunity, make sure that you prepare thoroughly beforehand.

60 Be honest about past difficulties but focus on how you dealt with them.

PREPARING FOR A REVIEW

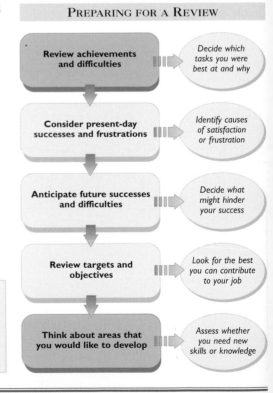

Review achievements and difficulties → *Decide which tasks you were best at and why*

Consider present-day successes and frustrations → *Identify causes of satisfaction or frustration*

Anticipate future successes and difficulties → *Decide what might hinder your success*

Review targets and objectives → *Look for the best you can contribute to your job*

Think about areas that you would like to develop → *Assess whether you need new skills or knowledge*

PARTICIPATING IN A PERFORMANCE REVIEW

Be as honest as you can about your achievements and areas for development during your appraisal. Keep an open mind about what may arise and try to react positively to feedback from your manager. Accept praise for any extra effort where it is due and listen carefully to any negative opinions. If you have prepared properly you will be able to describe your view of the situation. Try to elicit the learning points from any feedback. Summarize the main points of the appraisal and make sure that you act on any recommendations – your development needs to be driven by you.

61 Figure out in advance what you will say and how you will say it.

▼ DISCUSSING DEVELOPMENT

Envision how you would like to see your current role developing in the next year so that you can present a convincing case for any training needs.

Employee expresses wish to improve budgeting skills

Manager suggest formal training course

REVIEWING YOURSELF

If there is no organized review system at your workplace, or you work alone, set up the experience for yourself. You can make it as challenging as you like, but avoid using it as an excuse to tell yourself that everything is going well and that there is no action to take. You can work alone, or you can find someone you can trust to act as your sounding board. That person does not need to be familiar with your work. In fact, since the good relationship you have with a particular colleague can easily change, it is wisest to pick someone outside your workplace. Prepare your thoughts as you would for a normal review and talk or think through your answers. Write down your conclusions as a permanent record of this process for future reference.

DEVELOPING YOURSELF

You are responsible for your career development. Accept this responsibility and start making plans for your future development so that you can grow, learn, progress, and thrive in the employment market as well in your personal life.

62 Fulfill your work objectives and learn through self-development.

63 Think who might be prepared to act as your mentor.

64 Identify activities that suit the way you like to learn.

TAKING RESPONSIBILITY

Although you may get some help from enlightened employers in your career development, in the event that no assistance is forthcoming make sure that your own plans and hopes precede this. If you work for yourself or in a small group, you may feel that you cannot spare the time or money for your development, but to neglect it would be unwise. Without continuous attention to your development, even the most stimulating jobs can become stifling. Regular attention to this area will enrich both your work and your personal life.

BENEFITING FROM SELF-DEVELOPMENT

One advantage for people who take their own development seriously is that they are more confident about their own abilities. They are able to converse on a variety of subjects, seem more interested in others, and appear more interesting, too. If you have developed yourself by speaking to groups, for example, this will be revealed in your added poise when giving presentations. Being up to date on professional interests will make you a more attractive prospect to employers, and being knowledgeable about current affairs will be useful in any forum.

THINGS TO DO

1. Help yourself by reading books on aspects of management that interest you, such as motivating people or strategic thinking.
2. Enroll in some short courses that will take your knowledge further.
3. Read professional journals to keep abreast of new developments.

ENRICHING YOUR LIFE

Study is not necessarily dry, boring, or irrelevant. On the contrary, it can provide stimulation, excitement, and great leaps of understanding, but it does require hard work. If you find the right course, however, you will feel enriched by the experience. Bear in mind that development constitutes far more than formal studies. It includes all the activities that will broaden you as a person and accompany you through life. Think through areas that are ripe for development and aim to work on anything about which you feel unclear.

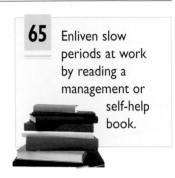

65 Enliven slow periods at work by reading a management or self-help book.

66 Think of ways to incorporate self-development into your career plan.

DOS AND DON'TS

✔ Do have a general idea of where your next job may be and the level at which you want work.

✔ Do plan now for what will make you suitable for the next job.

✔ Do act now to gain the knowledge you need for the next step.

✘ Don't underestimate the time needed to learn a new subject.

✘ Don't forget to explore learning opportunities that can be undertaken while working fulltime

✘ Don't neglect your development even if you feel satisfied at present.

◀ BEING PROACTIVE
By joining a local debating society, Neera made the most of a rare chance to learn a new skill and be given direct feedback on her performance. Without this valuable experience, she might have been held back at work by her unassertive attitude to speaking in public.

CASE STUDY
Neera decided that she wanted to develop her public speaking skills. Her job as a researcher did not call for any public speaking, and she knew that her employer would not sponsor her training, so she decided to look for some opportunities outside work. She did not want to restrict herself to studying the theory, she wanted practice and feedback on her areas for development. Through her local public library she found a debating society that met near her home. Although the first session was daunting, she found others there like herself. That was three years ago. She is now Secretary of the group. Although she feels she will never be a great orator, she can now speak with passion when needed. She has also found out how to structure a speech for maximum impact and how to use humor to hold an audience's attention.

GAINING KNOWLEDGE

Continual learning does not mean that you have to register for a new evening class every term. There are many other activities that contribute to our knowledge, such as coaching, mentoring, work shadowing, job sampling, exchanges, research activities, transfers, temporary appointments, or expanding an existing job into new areas. Much of what we learn is almost unconscious – picked up by watching, reading, and hearing about new ways of doing things. Always be on the lookout for new ways to develop your skills.

67 Realize that it is never too late to learn new skills.

68 Keep your computer skills up to date – seek out training at work.

69 Avoid being held back by a fear of the unknown.

BUILDING ON ACHIEVEMENTS

It is important to build on any previous investment in your development. If you have been on a course that you found interesting at the time or which you subsequently found useful, see if you can take this to the next stage with a more advanced course on the same subject. Alternatively, there may be allied subjects that you could study, either during working hours or outside work, that would provide you with further opportunities. If you have privately undertaken a course that has proved to be of benefit to you at work, consider whether your employers might support you in further training. If you can demonstrate the benefits, they might regard the cost as an investment.

◀ USING COMPUTER SOFTWARE
The ability to use information technology is a core skill that can apply to almost every job. Make sure that, at the very least, you keep up with the latest software packages and know how to use electronic mail.

IDENTIFYING METHODS OF LEARNING

METHOD	FACTORS TO CONSIDER
COACHING Working with a trainer or senior colleague to increase skills.	This is a good way of improving confidence and learning new skills on the job, particularly if you happen to be inexperienced or new to a role.
JOB SWAP Exchanging jobs with a colleague for a fixed period of time.	This enables you to experience different priorities, needs, and methods of working. For example, private and public sector accountants might do each other's work for a week.
MENTORING Being guided by an experienced colleague on a longer-term basis.	A mentoring relationship often runs for a minimum of 6 months and can be an invaluable experience, particularly when there is a high level of commitment on both sides.
READING Studying books, journals, articles, and researching on the internet.	Reading is a learning method that can easily be fitted into your spare time. Try to find a quiet spot where you can read at lunchtimes, such as in a library or park.
RESOURCE CENTERS Acquiring new skills at local or corporate access centers.	These centers can help you further your education, such as by learning a new language. Courses are very popular, so you may need to book in advance.
SABBATICAL Taking time off in order to study, travel, or do other work.	In academic life, sabbaticals are paid for once they have been fully justified, but this is rare in other sectors unless the break provides clear and necessary work input.
STUDY Participating in on-the-job training, courses, open learning, workshops.	Studying will help you progress in your career. Be aware, however, that the longer the course, the higher the level of application and commitment required.
TEMPORARY PROMOTION Working in a higher position until the position is filled permanently.	This enables you to gain experience working at a higher level and to decide whether the responsibility suits you. "Acting up" can lead to permanent promotion.
TRANSFER Moving temporarily to another post, department, or organization.	A short-term placement in an allied but different workplace offers variety and is a stimulating way to broaden experience and aid development.
WORK EXPERIENCE Gaining experience by doing paid or unpaid work for a period of time.	A formal placement involves trying out a role for a fixed period, often to a preset program. This is a chance to experience a different job first-hand.
WORK SHADOWING Accompanying someone who has a different job.	This is a useful way of seeing how someone else works. It provides an insight into their key tasks, related work practices, priorities, and problems.

Establishing Learning Groups

Managing other people can be isolating because it is difficult to truly be one of the team. Keep yourself motivated by establishing or joining a learning group, or learning set, so that you are able to rely on support and stimulation from your peers.

70 Make sure that all group members have the chance to contribute.

Defining Learning Groups

Increasing numbers of people who are interested in developing their own careers are setting up groups to plan, manage, and facilitate their own learning. Academic or professional issues can be considered and discussed, sometimes around real work problems that are affecting a member of the group. This allows true action learning: the objective consideration of the issue and possible solutions. These learning groups are run by groups of friends or colleagues who want to learn from and with each other, independent of any college or any work learning that may be taking place. Sometimes the group members will all be based in the same organization, but more often they will come from different places of work.

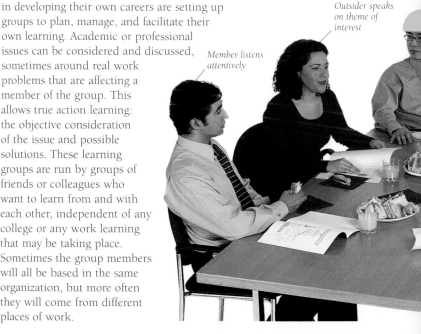

Outsider speaks on theme of interest

Member listens attentively

71 Prepare in advance to ensure thorough group discussion takes place.

ESTABLISHING A LEARNING GROUP

Form your own group from friends and associates. Try to pick a varied collection of people who will all have something special to contribute. They should possess similar outlooks and be interested in learning and helping each other to excel. Group members should initially commit to attending sessions for at least one year. Five or six people is plenty. Be open to others' needs: some people may be more interested in solving work problems or enhancing their employability; others may be seeking academic enrichment.

▼ RUNNING A LEARNING GROUP

Select a mix of people and discuss how you will work together. Ask guest speakers to attend, making sure that you cater to different styles and interests. Share good practice and learning events. Keep the atmosphere social and informal.

Member takes responsibility for running the meeting

Member asks a question on a point that concerns him

DOS AND DON'TS

✔ Do conduct regular reviews of your group's working procedures.

✔ Do make sure that everyone participates.

✔ Do tackle new subjects frequently.

✘ Don't have too many people from very similar backgrounds.

✘ Don't waste the time on general social chit-chat.

✘ Don't get too "safe" – introduce challenges.

Member sees how subject matter relates to her work situation

72 Discuss a wide range of subjects with your group.

73 Make sure that all members are accorded tolerance and respect.

ACHIEVING CAREER SUCCESS

As a career develops, twists and turns are inevitable. Be prepared to overcome obstacles, change direction when necessary, and turn events to your advantage so that you continue to thrive.

COPING WITH A SETBACK

Even with the most careful planning, career progression can sometimes be thrown off course by sudden, unexpected events. If you suffer a setback, keep calm, think positively, and plan what to do next so that you can reestablish your position.

74 Be aware of external changing circumstances that may affect you.

75 Note that a crisis can represent a turning point.

76 Adopt a calm approach to help diffuse a difficult situation.

RECOGNIZING THE CAUSES

We are all at the mercy of events over which we have little control. Common setbacks to a career include losing a job (perhaps due to being let go or being laid off), being demoted or moved to a new role (perhaps following a company merger or takeover), and failing to be promoted. Whatever the type of setback, it can result in a loss of dignity, demoralization, and damage to an individual's reputation. However, provided you handle such situations calmly and rationally, you can ensure that short-term obstacles do not affect your long-term prospects.

HANDLING SHORT-TERM SITUATIONS

SITUATION	IMPLICATIONS	ACTION
Loss of job provokes crisis leading to trauma and confusion.	May suffer lack of confidence, respond in an over-emotional way, and react by panicking.	Review your résumé, sound out employment agencies, plan the next step.
Merger or takeover creates difficult working environment and strains relationships.	Longer-term career ideas may be disrupted, requiring re-evaluation of your plans.	Consult a career counselor to review your future options before making any move.
Circumstances alter – perhaps the working brief changes or company fortunes fall.	Longer-term career ideas may need revising in the light of the current situation.	Keep abreast of changes, and monitor economic forces and vacancies in your field.

POINTS TO REMEMBER

- A setback is soon forgotten, but the way you reacted may not be.
- Suffering one setback after another could indicate that there is a mismatch between your career plans and reality.
- Keep a sense of perspective – work is just work and no one is indispensable.

77 Use the people you respect as sounding boards.

RESCUING THE SITUATION

Keep positive, look at all the facts, and see if you can find a way to get back on your original path or identify a new one. Analyze what caused a setback and try to take remedial action, such as putting progressive proposals to your superior. If you feel that you acted unwisely, try to undo any damage that you can. If you feel demoralized, perhaps as a result of having to leave work suddenly, look for ways to boost your confidence in other areas of your life while you think about your next move.

**REGAINING ▶
YOUR COMPOSURE**

Working on practical issues with colleagues can help to distract you from a difficult situation and maintain a sense of proportion until you decide what to do.

Team member is asked to give an update

IDENTIFYING THE NEED FOR CHANGE

There are times in every career when it is necessary to change direction. Keep checking that your original career plan is relevant as you develop and gain experience, and recognize the need to alter course if your circumstances or expectations change.

78 Anticipate change so that you can plan how to cope with it.

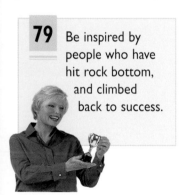

79 Be inspired by people who have hit rock bottom, and climbed back to success.

LOOKING BACK

It is important to compare what you are doing now with what you did before to see how you have changed and how your expectations and ambitions have progressed. You may have changed in ways that you had not anticipated, with the result that your original long-term career plans are no longer relevant. For example, if you have developed far more confidence after giving many presentations, you might want to take on a more visible role. Or perhaps you have discovered a new talent and would like to exploit it.

BEING PRACTICAL

Taking a new career path becomes more difficult the longer you leave it. In your 20s you are likely to have a "Why not?" attitude to drastic career changes. By your 30s you will be eager to establish yourself on a developing career path. Your 40s are likely to be your most ambitious years, while in your 50s starting a brand new career will seem highly risky. Once you have built up a track record and investment of time in one job area you will be loathe to relinquish it if that means starting all over again at the bottom of the ladder.

QUESTIONS TO ASK YOURSELF

Q Am I confident about the potential gains to be made?

Q Am I clear about the costs involved in the change?

Q Have I communicated with everyone who will be affected?

Q Have I considered possible disadvantages carefully?

Q Have I been realistic in my assessment and calculations?

EXAMINING REASONS FOR CHANGE

When a job is easy and every situation seems familiar, change is desirable. Staying in a position with no challenges can be stultifying. Perhaps you need more money or would work for less for more satisfaction. Health or family circumstances might be reasons for change or market depression or outlook could convince you to alter your plans. You may simply feel that you have outgrown your job and it has no more to offer you. Even if you feel happy and secure, you may need to change as a result of internal restructuring or a new appointment.

80 Plan for the future to give you a head start in anticipating change.

MAKING A ▶ POSITIVE CHANGE
Roger was happy in his work but wanted to see more of his family. Rather than change jobs, he made a convincing case for flexible working hours.

CASE STUDY
Roger was becoming resentful of the long hours he was required to work. He wanted to see more of his wife and two children. He approached his departmental head with the proposal that he try out flexible working for a trial period of one year. This would involve him working one less day a week but to compensate he would have to do some work at home and work longer hours on the days that he came into the office. His employers agreed but only to a six-month trial initially. They voiced concerns that the change in his working hours might jeopardize production. However, everything worked well and the flexible pattern continued for five years. The company then decided to open up similar opportunities to all staff to recognize the need for them to be able to adapt to the changing roles facing them outside work.

POINTS TO REMEMBER

● Change is normal and desirable. A static situation is a far greater cause for concern.

● Common reasons for changing career are to earn a larger salary or have better working conditions.

● While change can provide fresh ways to work, new ideas, and stimulating contacts, new routines take time to learn and it can be difficult to rethink old habits.

UNDERSTANDING BOTH SIDES OF CHANGE

Before deciding whether to make a change, weigh the benefits and disadvantages impartially. Discuss the issues with other people to help you think them through. For example, if you want to enjoy more flexible working hours, perhaps due to family commitments, you may have to accept that you will receive less financial reward. If you cannot progress any further in your current role without retraining, would it be worthwhile enrolling in a distance learning course?

ENHANCING YOUR PROSPECTS

*P*eople who strive to broaden their experience are attractive to employers. Consider taking time off for study, research, or travel, look for wider responsibilities in your present role, or aim to move to new pastures in order to enhance your prospects.

81 Change perspective by working in different areas of an organization.

QUESTIONS TO ASK YOURSELF

Q What could I do with a six-month career break? Could I specialize in a new area?

Q Is there an area of interest for me to research or study?

Q Would a work break give me any new skills that would be of value to my employer?

Q Would traveling be an option, and what are the likely costs?

Q Could I survive without pay for this period?

BROADENING KNOWLEDGE

Taking time off to study or travel is known as a sabbatical or a career break. In academic life, taking a sabbatical for research or study is common, and this concept of time out to replenish professional enthusiasm and knowledge is now gaining ground in other sectors. However, not all employers will look favorably on a request for a career break, since it may be costly to keep a post open. If this is the case with your employer, decide whether you could self-finance an unpaid work break. Alternatively, consider leaving your current job and taking a break before applying for another.

TAKING ON NEW ▶ CHALLENGES
This scenario depicts two outcomes for a team leader who became demotivated at work. By following outside interests, he developed his organizational skills and gained fresh confidence and enthusiasm. This was noticed when he returned to work and he was given a more challenging role. A failure to take action led him to feel more demotivated and depressed.

Team leader receives negative feedback in his review

Team leader becomes demotivated and despondent

CHANGING YOUR JOB PROFILE

If you are dissatisfied with your job, or if you are doing it because you need to, rather than because you want to, look for other areas to give you the extra sense of achievement that you are missing. Do you have an interest in other jobs in the organization? If so, why not offer to liaise between departments or sit on committees or project groups that could use your talents?

82 Consider taking on an extra element of responsibility – it may bring new interests and rewards.

THINGS TO DO

1. Evaluate your key work tasks and decide which are necessary, optional, or habitual.
2. Stop doing unnecessary tasks and break old habits.
3. Find different ways to perform necessary and optional tasks.
4. Work hard to acquire the right reputation and image.
5. Develop a positive outlook.

Relations with colleagues improve, and team leader is promoted to manager

Volunteers outside his work to help organize charity fund-raising events

Becomes more frustrated and isolated, damaging his career prospects

Continues in the same old routine

83 Make it a habit to try something different until it comes naturally.

84 Identify gaps in your life and try to find new ways of filling them.

KNOWING WHEN TO MOVE ON

Most jobs can become routine but sometimes you may feel as though you have ground to a halt. Perhaps you are desperate for each day to end because the work has become very predictable. Or perhaps you have stopped believing in what senior people say, or you have lost respect for the organization. Regularly assess how you feel about your job. Choose a subjective score from 0–10 where 0 = desperately bad and 10 = excellent. If you are frequently awarding your frame of mind lower than 5, you should consider changing your job. Consistently low scores show that you are having more negative than positive experiences. If your score is regularly at the top end of the scale, there is probably scope for you to stay in your job and make changes to improve your routine.

POINTS TO REMEMBER

● Don't wait until things have gone wrong before planning a change.

● It is always easier to get a job when you are employed than when you are out of work.

● A check needs to be kept on a changing situation – your second best option could become your preferred option in the longer term.

85 Change is a fact of life, so make sure that you plan to accommodate it.

86 Aim to leave a job that does not fulfill you before your morale suffers.

MAKING A FRESH START

If you feel unappreciated, or the essential day-to-day work does not interest you, or you believe you are being victimized, you are likely to feel cynical and frustrated. Perhaps you have experienced personal clashes with people at work, or a run of difficulties in performance. Even if these situations are not of your own making, by staying put you risk creating a bad atmosphere for everyone. You will also start to feel negative and alienated and become worn down and depressed. The best way forward is to cut your losses, move on, and make a fresh start somewhere new.

Receives a letter for a job interview

◀ **TAKING POSITIVE ACTION**
Staying in a job where you feel unhappy will harm your career, so start looking and applying for other jobs as soon as possible. Simply taking some positive action will put you in a better frame of mind.

REMAINING POSITIVE

Always talk positively about your current job in subsequent job interviews. Most interviewers are able to identify a demotivated candidate who is desperate to leave a job, even if you try to hide your true feelings in your answers. Avoid showing any lack of enthusiasm in the way you describe your current job, since a candidate who disparages his or her current employer will sound disloyal and give the impression that they will do the same about any future employer later on. Even if you feel you have been at a standstill, try to reinterpret your frustration by highlighting your achievements. Be as objective as you can and concentrate on what you learned. Discuss areas where you did feel that you contributed and explain why. Talk about where you would like to be heading rather than what you are anxious to leave behind.

87 Find positive aspects of your last job to discuss in an interview.

▼ BEING INTERVIEWED

Be positive about your last job when talking to prospective employers. If you are critical or negative of your colleagues or the organization, you risk giving the impression that you are untrustworthy

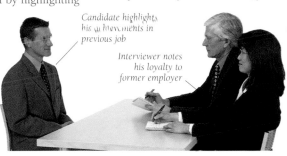

Candidate highlights his achievements in previous job

Interviewer notes his loyalty to former employer

88 Use the people you respect as sounding boards.

89 Think how to put the best spin on the job you want to leave.

DOS AND DON'TS

✔ Do be positive and enthusiastic – stress what you have to contribute in the future rather than on past disappointments.

✔ Do treat each new opportunity as a blank page.

✔ Do analyze your behavior on a regular basis.

✘ Don't develop an antagonistic or a cynical attitude.

✘ Don't get demoralized – a much more suitable job may be just around the corner.

✘ Don't dwell on your difficulties – in years to come you will struggle to remember what you were worrying about.

MAKING A CAREER MOVE

Waiting until a career decision is clear-cut can mean waiting forever. Assess the outcome of a move on a balance of probable gains and losses. Analyze what these mean to you to establish the important aspects of the options facing you.

90 Make a list of things you want from a job, then aim to get them.

QUESTIONS TO ASK YOURSELF

Q Have I established the salary, working hours, and conditions?

Q Are there any other benefits or any disadvantages?

Q What is the potential for progress up the career ladder?

Q Am I worried about how I would fit into a new kind of organization?

Q Would finding out more allay my fears?

BALANCING GAINS AND LOSSES

When you need to weigh up the advantages and disadvantages of making a career move, the quantitative factors that can be compared and contrasted are few. Having established the amount of pay, working hours, and conditions, plus daily commuting implications, the rest is simply a matter of adjudication about the quality of the benefits on offer. Use a combination of instinct, imagination, and judgment to find your way to a satisfactory outcome.

◄ ACHIEVING CLARITY
Penny needed to be clear about what she really wanted from her career. Armed with this information, she was able to make sensible decisions according to her real priorities. Without this clarity, Penny could have found that each job move brought more frustration than satisfaction, and her career direction may well have become confused.

CASE STUDY
Penny was very clear about what she wanted from her career. She had summarized her key motivational factors as being attention, achievement, and acclaim. For the past 5 years Penny had been moving toward a job where she felt fulfilled in each of these aspects. Her current role gave her the satisfaction of two of the three, but she felt it was time to find a new position that would offer her more.

Penny applied for a job and was invited to an interview. She found that having a clear vision of what she wanted helped her talk her way through the grueling interview process. When the company offered her the job, they said that a deciding factor was the clarity with which she could express herself and her goals. Weighing the new role, Penny found that the benefits to be gained outweighed any worries, and accepted the position.

91 Trust your instincts – what were your first feelings about an issue?

USING YOUR INSTINCT

Innate impulses, often called instincts, are immediate responses to act in one way or another. Recognize these powerful feelings, note them, and then examine what might have provoked them. Sometimes they are identifying subtle indicators that cause you discomfort or interest you. Try to articulate exactly what it is that you are feeling. Perhaps talking to someone about a proposed move would help you gain clarity about the relative advantages and disadvantages?

ASSESSING TANGIBLES

Tangible factors – those that can be measured or observed – include the physical conditions relating to a job and the policies practiced in an organization. Consider the salary, even if this is not your primary motivating factor, along with any other payments such as overtime, bonuses, expenses, pension contributions, or other financial incentives. The whole financial package should feel like the right rate for the job and the amount that you would need in order to accept the position. Other conditions to consider are working hours, travel time, opportunities for flexible working, and vacation arrangements.

92 Wait for written confirmation of a job offer before you resign.

POINTS TO REMEMBER

- Most people become set in their ways and need to be encouraged to try something different.
- Every change will have both pluses and minuses.
- Any decision to move should be based on objective factors rather than on whim.
- Making assumptions should be avoided – always check that the situation is really as you perceive it to be.

◀ **ASSESSING PRIORITIES**
Think carefully about the tangible factors of a career that are important to you. Being able to work part-time from home to reduce travel time may be a strong consideration for you.

LOOKING AT INTANGIBLES

There are also intangible factors to take into account when assessing a career change. These include the working atmosphere, the team approach, how an organization is run, quality of leadership, and career potential. Assess these by talking to staff who already work for the company. These factors, such as how motivating the environment would be, are almost completely subjective. You may only judge factors in this group, such as the degree of responsibility offered, how far creativity is encouraged, and how clearly communication takes place, from the interaction you have with a company prior to employment.

93 Assess whether the atmosphere in an organization feels right to you.

94 Weigh tangibles and intangibles before making career decisions.

Explains that job involves working some unsocial hours

Friend talks about her experience of shift work

◀ TALKING THROUGH YOUR OPTIONS

If you are finding it difficult to make a decision, talk through your concerns with a trusted friend. Ask them what they would do in your shoes. They may be able to point out considerations that you have so far overlooked.

CASE STUDY

Abbi, a senior social worker, loved her work. She felt valued, useful, and enjoyed the challenges of the job. However, after having children, the demands and the long hours proved exhausting. These feelings did not diminish when the children started school. At 45, Abbi decided to change her career in order to find working hours that fit in with her domestic priorities. She applied for a retraining grant and enrolled in college to become a teacher. Although she was sacrificing her seniority and higher salary, she was gaining more control over factors she viewed as important. Most significantly, even though the course was hard work, she started to enjoy life again, knowing that her professional skills were helping people while she was doing justice to her other priorities. She taught for 15 years until she retired and never regretted her change of career direction.

◀ CHANGING CAREER

After having a family, Abbi found that her career priorities changed. The benefits she gained from having more control over her working day far outweighed the higher status and salary she had previously enjoyed.

PLANNING A CAREER CHANGE

KEY ISSUES	HOW TO PLAN EFFECTIVELY

YOUR ROLE AND RESPONSIBILITY
What you expect and what is expected of you.

- Find out to what extent your skills are in demand in the marketplace. Take steps to update skills or acquire them if it would increase your options.
- Consider how you would sell your achievements and experience to an employer in a new field.

SALARY
Pay, overtime, bonuses, expenses, pension contributions.

- If it is likely that you would have to take a cut in salary, establish what your minimum income could be.
- Assess whether there is scope for achieving the level of financial reward you will need and want in the future – is there a ceiling that you need to be aware of?

CONDITIONS
Hours, flexible working, vacation time, work environment.

- Think about which conditions are most important to you – are you looking for similar or much better conditions than you have at present?
- If a change will involve working longer hours to learn the ropes, are you happy to make this commitment?

LOCATION
The place, or places, where you can expect to be based.

- If you make a big change, such as from administrative to technical work, the location may shift accordingly to become site-based rather than office-bound.
- Jobs that involve travel, especially on short notice, could prove difficult if you have family commitments.

CULTURE
Atmosphere, quality of leadership, staff attitudes, and team spirit.

- Decide which intangible aspects of a workplace, such as how it feels to work there, are most important to you.
- Profit-making or nonprofit organizations have different explicit goals and implicit values that you may want to take into account.

PROSPECTS
Will there be plenty of opportunity to move up the career ladder?

- If you are moving to enhance your future prospects, you will need to monitor your progress as you find your feet.
- Assess where you want to be in 5 years' time and find out if it is feasible to get there by changing career.

SURVIVING AND THRIVING

There are times when you will feel as though you are merely surviving at work. At other times you may feel that you are forging ahead. Learn how to handle the ups and downs of your career so that you stay on course for success.

95 Learning from failure can be just as useful as learning from success.

STAYING ON COURSE

From time to time you will be faced with circumstances, at work or at home, that may not be to your liking. These ups and downs need not throw you off course if you keep a positive mental attitude. Take the long view about progress at work to help you get through frustrating times. Short-term stagnation may be necessary for a later breakthrough. If work is frustrating, aim for successes in other areas of your life to help you feel calm and positive. Get some physical exercise. This will help you cope with pressure at work so that you can survive until you start to thrive again.

Team leader asks for feedback

Manager points out areas of improvement

◀ LEARNING FROM OTHERS
Discuss work with respected colleagues or peers and ask for advice when you are unsure how to proceed. It can be valuable to learn how people with different skills and experience might approach a problem.

96 Be prepared to ask for support from colleagues and to give them support.

EXPLORING ▶ NEW AREAS

Graham still had a lot to offer as he neared retirement. His willingness to work without pay at the end of his paid employment meant that his career continued to develop. He used his technical and managerial expertise to work in an entirely different setting for the good of others, a rewarding encounter which led him to further new experiences.

CASE STUDY

Graham, a water engineer, was nearing retirement but did not feel ready to stop work. He approached a volunteer organization that sent professionals overseas to see if they would be interested in someone of his age. To his delight, they were particularly eager to interview him because of his wealth of experience, which they realized was so badly needed in the developing world. He discovered that more than 300 of the 1,000 people they sent overseas were over 50. Six months later, Graham began a two-year placement on a water infrastructure project in a small African country. Working with the local community, he helped them improve drinking water and irrigation systems throughout the area. He returned home after extending his stay for a year and now gives talks to new volunteers to share his enthusiasm for and experience of such projects.

---

97 If you want to be able to enjoy a happy, fulfilled retirement, start planning for it early.

PLANNING AHEAD

These days it is not unusual for people to work until they are 70 or more. This does not mean that they continue in the same job. The usual retirement age of around 60 to 65 often spurs people to change priorities for the active years ahead. Your career priorities will change at different stages of your life. In your 20s you can afford to explore varied jobs and roles and consider professional training courses. In your 30s you may have family commitments. In your 40s you will want to be consolidating your progress, and in your 50s you are likely to be reaping the rewards of earlier education and training. At 60 you may be looking ahead, perhaps even thinking about a new direction. Your career plan needs to cover these different steps in your life, which means looking ahead and reviewing progress regularly.

CULTURAL DIFFERENCES

If you plan to work abroad, bear in mind the differences between cultures. In the United States and the Far East, for example, staff are usually given two weeks' paid vacation per year, whereas in Europe, approximately four to five weeks' paid leave is the norm. Permits may be needed to enable you to work legally in some countries, and most countries require that foreign workers pay taxes.

98 Keep checking that your career and life goals tally.

INVESTING IN OTHERS

The most effective managers are as interested in developing their teams as they are in their own progress. Encourage team members to manage their own careers by explaining your own approach and the benefits to be gained from good planning.

99 Use your own career planning skills to help and inspire others.

100 Develop staff and you will improve their effectiveness.

DEVELOPING STAFF

In addition to managing their own careers, good managers encourage their staff to take their career planning seriously. Whether your organization is large or small, or located in the public or private sector, other people in your team will benefit from your approach to career management. Talk to your team about how you manage your own career, and raise the subject at staff meetings. Highlight the benefits of people taking on new projects or moving into a new area. For example, you could stress how an individual might improve their career prospects by taking on work that would likely lead to a promotion. In this way staff can be inspired to welcome change and fully endorse any new developments.

USING PROJECT SKILLS ▼
Promote the discipline of project management so that team members learn to focus on priorities, monitor progress, overcome difficulties, and adapt to change. These skills can then be transferred to planning their individual improvement and development in consultation with you.

Team leader reports on progress of project

Manager encourages regular reviews

ENCOURAGING TEAMWORK

The more you explain to your team the benefits of career planning and make the link between development and performance, the more you will build an atmosphere that encourages development and learning. Provide opportunities for sharing learning with others and make time to discuss staff progress. Give priority to career subjects and promote self-development for all staff. Encourage team members to analyze their performance together and to highlight development activities that could improve their work in the future. In this way you will build team spirit and ensure that staff are positive and productive.

BEING AN EFFECTIVE ROLE MODEL ▼
Your behavior will have a direct effect on every member of every team you lead. Make sure that you always act positively to show that career success is worth working for.

 101 Reward good work and celebrate innovation to inspire your team to career success.

WEAK MANAGEMENT | STRONG MANAGEMENT

Does not share learning with staff

Shares learning and feedback with staff

Brushes aside career questions

Gives priority to discussing careers

Takes no interest in staff development

Positively encourages staff development

Does not help staff appraise themselves

Helps staff to monitor their own progress

ASSESSING YOUR CAREER MANAGEMENT SKILLS

Find out whether you are managing your career successfully by reading the following statements, and then choosing the option that is closest to your experience. If your answer is "never," circle Option 1; if it is "always," circle Option 4, and so on. Be honest with yourself. Add your scores together and refer to the analysis to see how you scored. Use your answers to identify areas that need improvement.

OPTIONS
1 Never
2 Occasionally
3 Frequently
4 Always

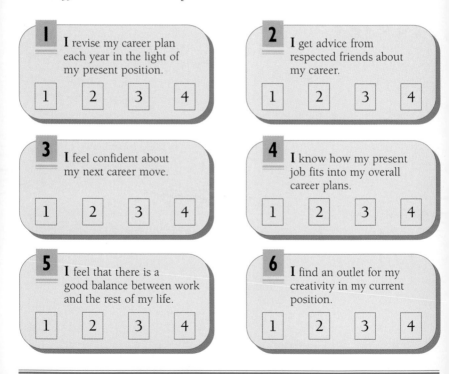

1 I revise my career plan each year in the light of my present position.

1 2 3 4

2 I get advice from respected friends about my career.

1 2 3 4

3 I feel confident about my next career move.

1 2 3 4

4 I know how my present job fits into my overall career plans.

1 2 3 4

5 I feel that there is a good balance between work and the rest of my life.

1 2 3 4

6 I find an outlet for my creativity in my current position.

1 2 3 4

7 The different parts of my life seem to fit together well.

1 2 3 4

8 I analyze my previous career moves and decisions.

1 2 3 4

9 I keep up to date with the current state of the employment market.

1 2 3 4

10 I network with friends and associates so that I hear about vacancies.

1 2 3 4

11 I work with others to keep my skills current and topical.

1 2 3 4

12 In each post I work at building my skills for the next one.

1 2 3 4

13 I am often involved in some type of formal learning activity.

1 2 3 4

14 I work out what I can contribute to each position I apply for.

1 2 3 4

15 I thoroughly research each new position available.

1 2 3 4

16 I use the internet to help me with research into employment issues.

1 2 3 4

17 I make a note of any achievements and successes when they occur.

1 2 3 4

18 I plan for performance reviews and make full notes in advance of the event.

1 2 3 4

19 I try to grasp the learning points of any career disasters.

1 2 3 4

20 I try to learn from disappointments and keep a positive frame of mind.

1 2 3 4

21 I resist moaning and avoid becoming cynical about my job.

1 2 3 4

22 I am a supportive colleague to my peers, superiors, and subordinates.

1 2 3 4

23 I often read a journal that is relevant to my profession.

1 2 3 4

24 I am a member of my relevant professional or trade association.

1 2 3 4

25 I regularly read a quality newspaper, including the business pages.

1 2 3 4

26 I work hard because I am ambitious to fulfill my goals.

1 2 3 4

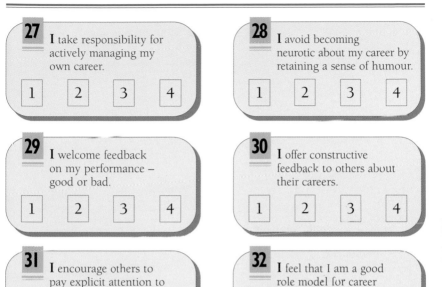

27 I take responsibility for actively managing my own career.

1   2   3   4

28 I avoid becoming neurotic about my career by retaining a sense of humour.

1   2   3   4

29 I welcome feedback on my performance – good or bad.

1   2   3   4

30 I offer constructive feedback to others about their careers.

1   2   3   4

31 I encourage others to pay explicit attention to their career management.

1   2   3   4

32 I feel that I am a good role model for career management.

1   2   3   4

ANALYSIS

Now that you have completed the self-assessment, add up your total score and check your career management skills by referring to the evaluation below. Identify your weakest areas and then reread relevant sections to help you further refine your skills.

32–64: You have a passive approach to your working life and are allowing career opportunities to slip away. Develop a clearer view of where you want to get to and make realistic plans of how to get there.

65–95: You are managing your career reasonably well but could afford to take more control of the factors affecting you.

96–128: You enjoy developing your career and it shows, but do keep your mind open to the unexpected opportunities that life can produce.

INDEX

ACKNOWLEDGMENTS

AUTHOR'S ACKNOWLEDGMENTS

This book is a result of effective team working. In particular I would like to thank Adèle Hayward for asking me to write the book; Jacky Jackson for her editorial expertise, insight, and focus, and Amanda Lebentz and the design team. Special thanks go to B, Robin, and other friends and clients who provided the inspiration.

PUBLISHER'S ACKNOWLEDGMENTS

Dorling Kindersley would like to thank the following for their help and participation in producing this book:

Photographer Matthew Ward

Models Dale Buckton, Angela Cameron, Mahesh Kanani, Aziz Khan, Kaz Takabatake, Suki Tan, Peter Taylor, Dominica Warburton, Silvana Viera.

Make-up Janice Tee, Paulin Hudson.

Picture research Anna Bedewell.
Picture librarian Melanie Simmonds.

Indexer Hilary Bird.

PICTURE CREDITS

Key: *a* above, *b* bottom, *c* centre, *l* left, *r* right, *t* top
Corbis Stock Market: 12bl; **Eyewire:** 46bl;
Photodisc: 32bl, 59bl; **Stone/Getty Images:** 4.

All other images © Dorling Kindersley.
For further information see: www.dkimages.com

AUTHOR'S BIOGRAPHY

Rebecca Tee is a leading expert in career management, presentation skills, and organizational development. A former president of the National Institute of Career Guidance in the UK, she advises individuals and companies on career issues and personal change. Rebecca is in demand as a conference speaker, trainer, and coach. Writing as Rebecca Corfield, she is the author of several bestselling titles, including *Preparing Your Own CV* and *Successful Interview Skills*.